Boobies:
A Calculator Dictionary

Compiled by Andrew Drummond

Published by I AM A STUDIO/ iamastud.io

ISBN 978-1-4478-4971-1

RIGHT WAY UP CALCULATOR

B	I	O	S	Z
8	1	0	5	2

Bi
81

Bib
818

Bibs
8185

Bibb
8188

Bibbs
81885

Bio
810

Bios
8105

Bis
815

Biz
812

Bo
80

Bos
805

Bob
808

Bobs
8085

Boo
800

Boos
8005

Boob
8008

RIGHT WAY UP CALCULATOR

B	I	O	S	Z
8	1	0	5	2

Boobs
80085

Booboo
800800

Booboos
8008005

Boss
8055

Bozo
8020

Bozos
80205

Ibis
1815

Io
10

Ios
105

Is
15

Iso
150

Isos
1505

Ob
08

Obs
085

Obi
081

Obis
0815

RIGHT WAY UP CALCULATOR

B I **O S** Z
8 1 **0 5** 2

Obo
080

Obos
0805

Oi
01

Oo
00

Oos
005

Os
05

Si
51

Sis
515

Sib
518

Sibs
5185

Siss
5155

So
50

Sos
505

Sob
508

Sobs
5085

Soss
5055

RIGHT WAY UP CALCULATOR

B I O S **Z**
8 1 0 5 **2**

Zizz
2122

Zo
20

Zos
205

Zoo
200

Zoos
2005

Be
38

Bes
538

Bee
338

Bees
5338

Beg
638

Begs
5638

Beige
36138

Beiges
536138

Beigel
736138

Beigels
5736138

Bel
738

Bels
5738

Belie
31738

Belies
531738

Bell
7738

Bells
57738

UPSIDE DOWN CALCULATOR

B E G H I L O S Z
8 3 6 4 1 7 0 5 2

Belle
37738

Belles
537738

Bellies
5317738

Besiege
3631538

Besieges
53631538

Bez
238

Bezel
73238

Bezels
573238

Bezes
53238

Bi
18

Bis
518

Bib
818

Bibs
5818

Bibb
8818

Bibbs
58818

Bible
37818

UPSIDE DOWN CALCULATOR

B E G H I L O S Z
8 3 6 4 1 7 0 5 2

Bibles
537818

Bibliologies
53160701 7818

Big
618

Bigs
5618

Bigg
6618

Biggs
56618

Biggie
316618

Biggies
5316618

Biggish
4516618

Bigos
50618

Bilbies
5318718

Bilbo
08718

Bilbos
508718

Bilboes
5308718

Bile
3718

Biles
53718

UPSIDE DOWN CALCULATOR

B	E	G	H	I	L	O	S	Z
8	3	6	4	1	7	0	5	2

Bilge
36718

Bilges
536718

Bill
7718

Bills
57718

BilliBi
18.17718

Billie
317718

Billies
5317718

Bio
018

Bios
5018

Biog
6018

Biogs
56018

Biologies
531607018

Bise
3518

Bish
4518

Bishes
534518

Biz
218

UPSIDE DOWN CALCULATOR

B E G H I L O S Z
8 3 6 4 1 7 0 5 2

Bize
3218

Bizzes
532218

Bleb
8378

Blebs
58378

Bless
55378

Blesses
5355378

Bliss
55178

Blisses
5355178

Blissless
553755178

Blob
8078

Blobs
58078

Blooie
310078

Bo
08

Bos
508

Bob
808

Bobs
5808

2 5 0 7 1 4 6 3 **8**
Z S O L I H G E **B**

UPSIDE DOWN CALCULATOR

Bobbies
5318808

Bobble
378808

Bobbles
5378808

Bobsleigh
461375808

Bobsleighs
5461375808

Bog
608

Bogs
5608

Boggish
4516608

Boggle
376608

Boggles
5376608

Bogie
31608

Bogies
531608

Bogle
37608

Bogles
537608

Boh
408

Boho
0408

Bohos
50408

Boil
7108

Boils
57108

Bole
3708

Boles
53708

Boll
7708

Bolls
57708

Bolo
0708

Bolos
50708

Bolshie
3145708

Bolshies
53145708

Boo
008

Boos
5008

Boob
8008

Boobs
58008

Boobies
5318008

UPSIDE DOWN CALCULATOR

B E G H I L O S Z
8 3 6 4 1 7 0 5 2

Boobish
4518008

Boobless
55378008

Booboisie
315108008

Booboisies
5315108008

Booboo
008008

Booboos
5008008

Boogie
316008

Boogies
5316008

Boohoo
004008

Boohoos
5004008

Bool
7008

Bools
57008

Booze
32008

Boozes
532008

Bosh
4508

Boshes
534508

UPSIDE DOWN CALCULATOR

B E G H I L O S Z
8 3 6 4 1 7 0 5 2

Boss
5508

Bosses
535508

Bossies
5315508

Bozo
0208

Bozos
50208

Ebb
883

Ebbs
5883

Ee
33

Eel
733

Eels
5733

Egg
663

Eggs
5663

Eggless
5537663

Eggshell
77345663

Eggshells
577345663

Egis
5163

UPSIDE DOWN CALCULATOR

B **E** G H I L O S Z
8 **3** 9 4 1 7 0 5 2

Egises
535163

Ego
063

Egos
5063

Egoless
5537063

Eh
43

Ehs
543

Eisegeses
535363513

Eisegesis
515363513

El
73

Els
573

Elegies
5316373

Elegise
3516373

Elegises
53516373

Elegize
3216373

Elegizes
53216373

Elhi
1473

UPSIDE DOWN CALCULATOR

B	**E**	G	H	I	L	O	S	Z
8	**3**	6	4	1	7	0	5	2

Eligible
37816173

Eligibles
537816173

Ell
773

Ells
5773

Else
3573

Es
53

Eses
5353

Esile
37153

Ess
553

Esses
53553

Esse
3553

Gebel
73836

Gee
336

Gees
5336

Geese
35336

Geez
2336

UPSIDE DOWN CALCULATOR

B E G H I L O S Z
8 3 6 4 1 7 0 5 2

Gel
736

Gels
5736

Gelee
33736

Gelees
533736

Gellies
5317736

Geo
036

Geos
5036

Geologies
531607036

Geologise
351607036

Geologises
5351607036

Geologize
321607036

Geologizes
5321607036

Gesso
05536

Gessoes
5305536

Ghee
3346

Ghees
53346

UPSIDE DOWN CALCULATOR

B E **G** H I L O S Z
8 3 **6** 4 1 7 0 5 2

Ghi
146

Ghis
5146

Ghibli
178146

Ghiblis
5178146

Ghillie
3177146

Ghillies
53177146

Gi
16

Gis
516

Gib
816

Gibs
5816

Gibe
3816

Gibes
53816

Gie
316

Gies
5316

Gig
616

Gigs
5616

UPSIDE DOWN CALCULATOR

B E **G** H I L O S Z
8 3 **6** 4 1 7 0 5 2

Giggle
376616

Giggles
5376616

Gigolo
070616

Gigolos
5070616

Gilgie
316716

Gilgies
5316716

Gill
7716

Gills
57716

Gillie
317716

Gillies
5317716

Gio
016

Glebe
38376

Glebes
538376

Glee
3376

Glees
53376

Gleg
6376

UPSIDE DOWN CALCULATOR

B E **G** H I L O S Z
8 3 **6** 4 1 7 0 5 2

Glei
1376

Gleis
51376

Glib
8176

Gliosis
5150176

Glob
8076

Globs
58076

Globe
38076

Globes
538076

Globose
3508076

Glogg
66076

Gloggs
566076

Gloss
55076

Glosses
5355076

Glossies
53155076

Glossologies
53160705 5076

Gloze
32076

UPSIDE DOWN CALCULATOR

B E **G** H I L O S Z
8 3 **6** 4 1 7 0 5 2

Glozes
532076

Go
06

Gob
806

Gobs
5806

Gobbi
18806

Gobble
378806

Gobbles
5378806

Gobbo
08806

Gobies
531806

Gobo
0806

Gobos
50806

Goboes
530806

Goes
5306

Goggle
376606

Goggles
5376606

Gogo
0606

UPSIDE DOWN CALCULATOR

B E **G** H I L O S Z
8 3 **6** 4 1 7 0 5 2

Gogos
50606

Gollies
5317706

Golosh
450706

Goo
006

Goos
5006

Google
376006

Googles
5376006

Googlies
53176006

Googol
706006

Googols
5706006

Goolie
317006

Goolies
5317006

Goose
35006

Gooses
535006

Goosegog
60635006

Goosegogs
560635006

UPSIDE DOWN CALCULATOR

B E **G** H I L O S Z
8 3 **6** 4 1 7 0 5 2

Gosh
4506

Gosse
35506

Gosses
535506

He
34

Hes
534

Hebe
3834

Hebes
53834

Heel
7334

Heels
57334

Heelless
55377334

Heh
434

Heigh
46134

Heil
7134

Heils
57134

Hele
3734

Heles
53734

UPSIDE DOWN CALCULATOR

B E **G** **H** I L O S Z
8 3 **6** **4** 1 7 0 5 2

Helios
501734

Hellish
4517734

Hell
7734

Hello
07734

Hells
57734

Hellos
507734

Heli
1734

Helloes
5307734

Helis
51734

Helo
0734

Helio
01734

Helos
50734

Hellhole
37047734

Hi
14

Hellholes
537047734

His
514

Hie
314

Hies
5314

Higgle
376614

Higgles
5376614

High
4614

Highs
54614

Highish
4514614

Hili
1714

Hill
7714

Hills
57714

Hillbillies
53177187714

Hillo
07714

Hillos
507714

Hiss
5514

Hisses
535514

Hissies
5315514

UPSIDE DOWN CALCULATOR

B	E	G	**H**	I	L	O	S	Z
8	3	6	**4**	1	7	0	5	2

Ho
04

Hos
504

Hob
804

Hobs
5804

Hobbies
5318804

Hobble
378804

Hobbles
5378804

Hobo
0804

Hobos
50804

Hoboes
530804

Hoe
304

Hoes
5304

Hog
604

Hogs
5604

Hogg
6604

Hoggs
56604

UPSIDE DOWN CALCULATOR

B E G **H** I L O S Z
8 3 6 **4** 1 7 0 5 2

Hoggish
4516604

Hoh
404

Hoi
104

Hoise
35104

Hole
3704

Holes
53704

Holeless
55373704

Holies
531704

Hollies
5317704

Hollo
07704

Holloes
5307704

Hols
5704

Hoo
004

Hoolie
317004

Hose
3504

Hoses
53504

UPSIDE DOWN CALCULATOR

B	E	G	**H**	I	L	O	S	Z
8	3	6	**4**	1	7	0	5	2

Hosel
73504

Hosels
573504

Hoss
5504

Hosses
535504

Ibis
5181

Ibises
535181

Igg
661

Iggs
5661

Igloo
00761

Igloos
500761

Ill
771

Ills
5771

Illegible
378163771

Io
01

Ios
501

Is
51

UPSIDE DOWN CALCULATOR

B	E	G	**H**	**I**	L	O	S	Z
8	3	6	**4**	**1**	7	0	5	2

Ish
451

Isle
3751

Isles
53751

Isleless
55373751

Iso
051

Isos
5051

Isogloss
55076051

Isoglosses
5355076051

Isohel
734051

Isohels
5734051

Isolog
607051

Isologs
5607051

Issei
13551

Isseis
513551

Lee
337

Lees
5337

UPSIDE DOWN CALCULATOR

B E G H I L O S Z
8 3 6 4 1 7 0 5 2

Leese
35337

Leg
637

Legs
5637

Leges
53637

Legge
36637

Legges
536637

Legible
3781637

Legless
5537637

Lei
137

Leis
5137

Les
537

Lesbo
08537

Lesbos
508537

Leses
53537

Less
5537

Lessee
335537

UPSIDE DOWN CALCULATOR

B E G H I **L** O S Z

8 3 6 4 1 **7** 0 5 2

Lessees
5335537

Lez
237

Lezes
53237

Lezz
2237

Lezzes
532237

Lezzie
312237

Lezzies
5312237

Li
17

Lis
517

Lib
817

Libs
5817

Libel
73817

Libels
573817

Libelee
3373817

Libelees
53373817

Libellee
33773817

UPSIDE DOWN CALCULATOR

B E G H I **L** O S Z
8 3 9 4 1 **7** 0 5 2

Libellees
533773817

Lie
317

Lies
5317

Liege
36317

Lieges
536317

Lig
617

Ligs
5617

Lilies
531717

Lilo
0717

Lilos
50717

Lisle
37517

Lisles
537517

Lisse
35517

Lo
07

Los
507

Lob
807

UPSIDE DOWN CALCULATOR

B E G H I **L** O S Z
8 3 6 4 1 **7** 0 5 2

Lobs
5807

Lobbies
5318807

Lobe
3807

Lobes
53807

Lobi
1807

Loblollies
5317707807

Lobo
0807

Lobos
50807

Lobolo
070807

Lobolos
5070807

Lobose
350807

Loess
55307

Log
607

Logs
5607

Loge
3607

Loges
53607

Loggie
316607

Loggish
4516607

Logie
31607

Logies
531607

Loglog
607607

Loglogs
5607607

Logo
0607

Logos
50607

Loll
7077

Lolls
57707

Lollies
5317707

Loo
007

Loos
5007

Loobies
5318007

Looie
31007

Looies
531007

UPSIDE DOWN CALCULATOR

B	E	G	H	I	**L**	O	S	Z
8	3	6	4	1	**7**	0	5	2

Loose
35007

Looses
535007

Lose
3507

Loses
53507

Losel
73507

Losels
573507

Loss
5507

Losses
535507

Ob
80

Obs
580

Obe
380

Obes
5380

Obeli
17380

Obelise
3517380

Obelises
53517380

Obelize
3217380

UPSIDE DOWN CALCULATOR

B E G H I **L** **O** S Z
8 3 6 4 1 **7** **0** 5 2

Obelizes
53217380

Obo
080

Obese
35380

Obos
5080

Obi
180

Oboe
3080

Obis
5180

Oboes
53080

Oblige
361780

Obol
7080

Obliges
5361780

Obols
57080

Obligee
3361780

Obole
37080

Obligees
53361780

Oboles
537080

UPSIDE DOWN CALCULATOR

B E G H I L O S Z
8 3 6 4 1 7 0 5 2

Oboli
17080

Obsess
553580

Obsesses
53553580

Oe
30

Oes
530

Ogee
3360

Ogees
53360

Ogle
3760

Ogles
53760

Oh
40

Ohs
540

Oho
040

Oi
10

Oil
710

Oils
5710

Ole
370

UPSIDE DOWN CALCULATOR

B E G H I L **O** S Z
8 3 6 4 1 7 **0** 5 2

Oleo
0370

Oleos
50370

Olio
0170

Ologies
5316070

Oo
00

Oos
500

Ooh
400

Oohs
5400

Oose
3500

Ooze
3200

Oozes
53200

Os
50

Ose
350

See
335

Sees
5335

Seel
7335

UPSIDE DOWN CALCULATOR

B	E	G	H	I	L	O	S	Z
8	3	6	4	1	7	0	5	2

Seels
57335

Seg
635

Sego
0635

Segos
50635

Sei
135

Seis
5135

Seil
7135

Seils
57135

Seise
35135

Seises
535135

Seize
32135

Seizes
532135

Sel
735

Seles
53735

Sell
7735

Sells
57735

UPSIDE DOWN CALCULATOR

B E G H I L O **S** Z
8 3 6 4 1 7 0 **5** 2

Selle
37735

She
345

Sese
3535

Shes
5345

Sess
5535

Sheesh
453345

Sesses
535535

Shell
77345

Sessile
3715535

Shells
577345

Sez
235

Sheol
70345

Sh
45

Sheols
570345

Shh
445

Shiel
73145

Shiels
573145

Shies
53145

Shigelloses
53507736145

Shigellosis
51507736145

Shill
77145

Shills
577145

Shoe
3045

Shoes
53045

Shoebill
77183045

Shoebills
577183045

Shoeless
55373045

Shog
6045

Shogs
56045

Shogi
16045

Shoo
0045

Shoos
50045

UPSIDE DOWN CALCULATOR

B E G H I L O **S** Z
8 3 6 4 1 7 0 **5** 2

Shoogle
3760045

Shoogles
53760045

Si
15

Sis
515

Sib
815

Sibs
5815

Siege
36315

Sieges
536315

Sigh
4615

Sighs
54615

Sigil
71615

Sigils
571615

Sigloi
107615

Siglos
507615

Sile
3715

Siles
53715

UPSIDE DOWN CALCULATOR

B E G H I L O **S** Z
8 3 6 4 1 7 0 **5** 2

Sill
7715

Sills
57715

Sillies
5317715

Silo
0715

Silos
50715

Sissies
5315515

Size
3215

Sizes
53215

Sizzle
372215

Sizzles
5372215

Slee
3375

Sleigh
461375

Sleighs
5461375

Slob
8075

Slobs
58075

Slobbish
45188075

UPSIDE DOWN CALCULATOR

B E G H I L O **S** Z

8 3 6 4 1 7 0 **5** 2

Sloe
3075

Sloes
53075

Slog
6075

Slogs
56075

Sloosh
450075

Slooshes
53450075

Slosh
45075

Sloshes
5345075

So
05

Sos
505

Sob
805

Sobs
5805

Sobole
370805

Soboles
5370805

Sog
605

Sogs
5605

UPSIDE DOWN CALCULATOR

8	3	6	4	1	7	0	**5**	2
B	E	G	H	I	L	O	**S**	Z

Soh
405

Soho
0405

Sohs
5405

Soil
7105

Soils
57105

Soilless
55377105

Sol
705

Sols
5705

Sole
3705

Soles
53705

Solei
13705

Soleless
55373705

Solgel
736705

Soli
1705

Solo
0705

Solos
50705

Ssh
455

Zee
332

Zees
5332

Zelos
50732

Zho
042

Zhos
5042

Zibo
0812

Zig
612

Zigs
5612

Zizz
2212

Zizzes
532212

Zo
02

Zos
502

Zoo
002

Zoos
5002

Zoologies
531607002

UPSIDE DOWN CALCULATOR

B E G H I L O S Z
8 3 6 4 1 7 0 5 2

90° CLOCKWISE CALCULATOR

A J N O W

6 7 2 0 3

Aa
66

Ajowan
670362

An
62

Ana
626

Anan
6262

Ann
622

Anna
6226

Anno
6220

Annona
622026

Anoa
6206

Anon
6202

Aw
63

Awa
636

Awn
632

90° CLOCKWISE CALCULATOR

A	J	N	O	W
6	**7**	**2**	0	3

Jann
7622

Jaw
763

Jawan
76362

Jnana
72626

Jo
70

Joanna
706226

Jow
703

Na
26

Naan
2662

Nan
262

Nana
2626

Nanna
26226

Naw
263

No
20

90° CLOCKWISE CALCULATOR

A J **N O W**

6 7 **2 0 3**

Non
202

Nona
2026

Noo
200

Noon
2002

Now
203

Nown
2032

On
02

Oon
002

Ow
03

Own
032

Wan
362

Wanna
36226

Waw
363

Wawa
3636

90° CLOCKWISE CALCULATOR

A J N O **W**
6 7 2 0 **3**

Wo
30

Won
302

Woo
300

Wow
303

90° COUNTER-CLOCKWISE CALCULATOR

A	J	M	N	O	R
9	4	3	2	0	7

Ajar
7649

Am
39

Ama
939

Amarna
927939

Amman
29339

Ammo
0339

Ammon
20339

Ammono
020339

Ar
79

Arar
7979

Arm
379

Armor
70379

Aroma
93079

Jam
394

Jar
794

Jomo
0304

Ma
93

Maa
993

Maar
7993

Major
70493

Mam
393

Mama
9393

Mamma
93393

Mammon
203393

90° COUNTER-CLOCKWISE CALCULATOR

A	**J**	**M**	N	O	R
9	**4**	**3**	2	0	7

Man
293

Mana
9293

Manana
929293

Manna
92293

Mannan
292293

Mano
0293

Manoao
090293

Manor
70293

Mar
793

Mara
9793

Marjoram
39704793

Marm
3793

Maroon
200793

Maror
70793

90° COUNTER-CLOCKWISE CALCULATOR

A	J	**M**	N	O	R
9	4	**3**	2	0	7

Marram
397793

Marrano
0297793

Marron
207793

Mm
33

90° COUNTER-CLOCKWISE CALCULATOR

A J **M** N O R
9 4 **3** 2 0 7

Mna
923

Mo
03

Moa
903

Moan
2903

Mojarra
9779403

Mojo
0403

Mom
303

Momma
93303

Mon
203

Mona
9203

Mono
0203

Moo
003

Moon
2003

Moor
7003

90° COUNTER-CLOCKWISE CALCULATOR

A	J	M	N	O	R
9	4	3	2	0	7

Moorman
2937003

Mor
703

Mora
9703

Mormaor
7093703

Mormon
203703

Morn
2703

Moron
20703

Morra
97703

Morro
07703

Naam
3992

Nam
392

Nom
302

Noma
9302

Nonmajor
70493202

Nor
702

Norm
3702

Norma
93702

Norman
293702

Oar
790

Om
30

Oom
300

Oor
700

Or
70

Ora
970

90° COUNTER-CLOCKWISE CALCULATOR

A	J	M	N	O	R
9	4	3	2	0	7

Orra
9770

Raj
497

Raja
9497

Ram
397

Ramona
920397

Ran
297

Rana
9297

Roam
3907

Roan
2907

Roar
7907

Rom
307

Roma
9307

Roman
29307

90° COUNTER-CLOCKWISE CALCULATOR

A	J	M	N	O	R
9	4	3	2	0	7

Romano
029307

Roo
007

Room
3007

www.ingramcontent.com/pod-product-compliance
Lightning Source LLC
Chambersburg PA
CBHW032103280526
45784CB00013B/3061
* 9 7 8 1 4 4 7 8 4 9 7 1 1 *